60 ONE-MINUTE
MARRIAGE-BUILDERS

Other books by Dave and Claudia Arp

Ten Dates for Mates by Dave and Claudia Arp. A self-help book, containing ten fun-packed dates to boost husband-wife communication. Thomas Nelson Publishers, 1983.

Sanity in the Summertime by Claudia Arp and Linda Dillow. A survival guide for mothers to build strong relationships with their children in the summer and all year long. Thomas Nelson Publishers, 1981.

Almost 13—Shaping Your Child's Teenage Years Today by Claudia Arp. Helping you get ready for the teen years and learning how to survive them. Thomas Nelson Publishers, 1986.

MOM's Support Group Video Package by Claudia Arp. Contains a five-part video series entitled **How to Suport Your Local Parents**, and a resource guide to assist in implementing the program. Published by Marriage Alive, 1988.

MOM's & DAD's Support Group Video Package by Dave and Claudia Arp. Contains a five-part video series, leader's resource guide and ten study guides for individual participants. Published by Marriage Alive, 1989.

60 ONE-MINUTE MARRIAGE-BUILDERS

Dave and Claudia Arp

ய

Wolgemuth & Hyatt, Publishers, Inc.
Brentwood, Tennessee

Wolgemuth & Hyatt, Publishers, Inc., P.O. Box 1941, Brentwood,
Tennessee 37027.

Printed in the United States of America.

Library of Congress Cataloging-in-Publication Data

Arp, Dave.
    60 one-minute marriage-builders / Dave and Claudia Arp. — 1st ed.
    p.   cm.
ISBN 0-943497-49-3
1. Marriage—Miscellanea. I. Arp, Claudia. II. Title.
III. Title: Sixty one-minute marriage-builders.
HQ734.A688   1989
646.7'8—dc19   89-5374

To David and Vera Mace,
our friends and our mentors.

CONTENTS

ACKNOWLEDGMENTS

Any attempt to list all who gave input would be incomplete. However, we especially want to acknowledge and express appreciation to the following:

Thanks to David and Vera Mace, who have been wonderful teachers and mentors and have modeled to us what a growing and healthy marriage looks like!

Thanks to the Association of Couples in Marriage Enrichment, founded by the Maces, and the ACME monthly publication that gave seed for many of our Minute-Builders. (For information about ACME write to P.O. Box 10596, Winston-Salem, NC 27108.)

Thanks to Paul and Leslie Lewis and their publication *Dad's Only* that has over the years fed good ideas for family fun to us and now on to our readers. (For information about *Dad's Only* write to P.O. Box 340, Julian, CA 92036.)

Thanks to Robert Wolgemuth and Mike Hyatt, our editors who expanded our horizons and encouraged us to pass our minute builders on to you!

Thanks to Lynne Attaway for her expertise and help in editing this series.

And thanks to our three sons, Jarrett, Joel and Jonathan for being our human "guinea pigs" and allowing us to share our family memories with you.

INTRODUCTION

Recently at a neighborhood party, a young wife asked in sheer frustration, "Can anybody tell me what a healthy marriage really looks like? I want to build my own marriage, but I don't know where to start."

This caused us to stop and reflect. What are the indicators of a healthy marriage? Certainly we would include commitment to the relationship, good communication, romance, being on the same team, and having common goals. But if we had to sum it up in a nutshell, we'd say, "A healthy marriage is one in which there is a willingness to work on the marriage relationship." Researchers agree with us. According to a recent poll of twelve thousand people, the number one cause of marriage breakups is the failure of partners to work at their marriage! Think about this—the number one cause of divorce is preventable! You can do something to insure that you are not a statistic! No one gets married and then plans to be a divorce statistic. But in today's fast-paced world, it's easy to let our marriage relationship slip. We took our own survey and asked people, "What is the number one reason couples don't work on their marriages?" The overwhelming answer we received was, "lack of time." It does take time for intimacy to develop and for relationships to grow—but it doesn't take big blocks of time. You can find time in little places. Minute by minute you can build your marriage!

We learned this the hard way. We've been working on our marriage for twenty-six years, and it hasn't always been easy. Before we had children, it was easier to find time for each other, but after having three boys in five years, we were slowly becoming strangers. We kept looking for a large block of time to clean the barnacles off our marriage ship, but you know the story—"We'll talk about that tomorrow—next month—next summer or next year!" It just didn't happen—until we moved to Europe! Part of our culture shock was getting used to being with each other! Suddenly, with a language barrier, no friends or family close by, and no busy schedule, we found the time we needed to work on our own relationship. It wasn't always easy, but one by one we began to chip away at the barnacles on our boat, and our marriage began to grow.

You may be thinking, "If we could move to the other side of the world and get away from all our responsibilities and pressures, we could work on our marriage too!" Here's good news for you: You don't have to have a lot of time to build your marriage. You don't have to have large blocks of time—but you do need some time. Why not look for it in the *little places*. And to help you do just that, we have put together this little book of *minute marriage-builders*. You have to start somewhere. While many of the marriage-builders are for couples to do together, there are also many you can do alone. Working on a relationship often starts with just one person, and since you are reading this book, guess who's elected—you! Start where you are. As you see new growth in your marriage, you'll be ready to move on to the next step. Remember, we learned these principles over a period of many years. If you try to do them all in the next month, you'll hate us, you'll hate your partner, and you'll hate yourself.

We suggest that you use this book once a week or twice a month. It is not a book to read straight through, but instead is a resource of simple, easy, and quick ideas that you can use to build your marriage. So whether you're a pre-married, newly-wed, or middle-aged couple, a dual-career or retired couple, let us encourage you to start today and use the little moments you do have to build a healthy and growing marriage.

What does a healthy marriage look like? If you use your *minutes* wisely and work on your marriage, you can answer our question by looking in your own marriage mirror. Picture that in your mind!

PART ONE

APPETIZERS

HOW MUCH DO YOU KNOW ABOUT YOUR MATE?

How much do you really know about your mate? Most couples tend to talk about everything except themselves, so you may be surprised to discover how much you don't know about your mate's personal likes and dislikes—no matter how long you've been married!

To discover what your mate is thinking and to find out personal preferences, play the game *TRY ME* in your spare moments together.

Either one of you starts the game. Ask a question about yourself which the other must try to answer, such as, "Tell me how I would spend an evening if I could do anything I wanted."

The game's purpose, of course, is to deepen your knowledge of each other. The subjects may range from heavy, "Tell me my position on nuclear disarmament," to light, "Tell me my favorite flavor of gum."

Here are some questions to get you started. Tell me:

1. One subject I would like to study.

2. Two comic strips I read regularly.

3. Which place I would visit first in a strange city—the museum or the shopping mall.

4. Who's the funniest person I know.

5. My favorite saying.

6. Which color I think I look best in.

Once you get started, you may have trouble stopping. At least you'll end the game with some new insights about your mate! Why not try it and find out for yourself?

WHY MARRIAGES
GO WELL

We know many reasons why marriages go sour, but what do healthy marriages really look like? Evelyn and Paul Mischetta decided to find out. They researched healthy marriages and published their results in their book, *Caring Couples*.

What do healthy marriages look like? Here are some of the results:

The Mischetta's found two distinct groups of couples. The first group were called the "naturals."

The naturals were equipped for intimacy in marriage because they had very positive childhoods. They had grown up in families with positive role models and with a spirit of cooperation.

The second group were the "learners." If you're in this group, you're in the majority. Learners have to work harder. They had less favorable childhoods and less favorable life experiences before marriage.

Now get this—the learners achieved the same high levels of marital growth as the naturals, but they used every means possible to grow in a positive way. Like the naturals, their marriages remained vibrant, alive, and exciting.

But it took hard work for both the learners and the naturals. Good marriages don't just happen. The Mischettas shared this insight: "Too many of us have a survival mentality. All that matters is self-interest, self-protection, and self-expression." Set aside that survival mentality and develop the relationship with your mate.

Remember, whether you're a natural or a learner, it takes work to be a winner. But it's really worth it. You can be a winner in your marriage!

THREE

CONTINUING THE COURTSHIP

Does the courtship have to end with the honeymoon? Our answer is emphatically NO! It is possible to continue the courtship through all the years of marriage. To keep the courtship alive, agree never to take each other for granted. Think back to your dating days. Remember that excited feeling you had as you were getting ready to go out with your special date? Remember how hard it was to say good night and how you just detested being apart? Thinking about the "olden days" may help us to appreciate our mates in the "here and now."

Take a couple of minutes right now. Decide on one practical thing you can do today to show your mate that he or she is special. What about giving your mate some words of appreciation? Demonstrate your gratitude in a practical way. Maybe you'll want to send a card or make a phone call or plan a special date. You could even re-create a date you had before you were married. Go back to that same "greasy spoon" or take that hike once again or rent the movie you saw on your first date. Let us encourage you to court your mate today.

The honeymoon can be the beginning, not the end, of romance in your marriage!

FOUR

DOES YOUR MARRIAGE NEED A FACE LIFT?

If you've been married several years, boredom and flatness may threaten your marital bonds. It may be time for a face lift. Remember, the marriage relationship is ever-changing. Your marriage is either growing and expanding or shrinking and withering.

Sometimes couples hesitate to reveal personal concerns that might trigger a conflict. But if you don't discuss what's bothering you, you perpetuate your dissatisfaction or emptiness. In one sense you become a "married split."

Let us encourage you to express how you really feel about things. Open expression will build an emotional investment in your marriage and keep communication alive. Even if some pain is involved, you can view it as a marriage face lift.

So whether you'd like some changes in menus, love making, or the way you spend Sunday afternoons, express how you feel rather than avoid each other. Just do it in the right way.

Try using "I" statements, and let the statement reflect back on you: "I feel a little bored when we spend most Sunday afternoons watching TV. Could we plan to do something different and creative next Sunday?"

In this way you can express yourself without attacking your mate as if you'd said, "You don't ever want to do anything but watch TV on Sunday afternoon!"

You'll probably always need to practice some give and take in living the everyday events. But being willing to live on the growing edge and to take a few risks will help eliminate boredom and flatness in your marriage.

So take the risk. . . . Start working on your marital face lift today!

FIVE

A GOOD MARRIAGE
HAS TWO LEARNERS!

Would you like to live on the growing edge of your marriage? An alive marriage is one in which both partners are learning and growing together. Are you a learner in your marriage?

Here's a checklist to see if you're learning or losing:

1. A learner says, "Let's find out." A loser says, "Nobody knows."

2. A learner who makes a mistake says, "I was wrong." A loser says, "It wasn't my fault!"

3. A learner goes through a problem. A loser goes around it.

4. A learner listens. A loser just waits for his turn to talk.

5. A learner explains. A loser explains away.

6. A learner knows what to fight for and what to compromise on. A loser compromises on what he shouldn't and fights for what's not worth fighting about.

7. A learner paces himself. A loser has two speeds—panicky and passive!

Remember, in marriage failures can be opportunities to learn. Be a learner in your marriage, and you'll be the winner!

DO THE UNEXPECTED

Good marriages don't stand still. They need to grow constantly or they will become stale. Current research testifies that many marriages go stale over time. Is your marriage growing or standing still? Actually, standing still is not really an option: If we're not growing in our marriages then we're probably becoming dry and flavorless.

Maybe you'd like to take a growth spurt in your marriage but just don't know where to begin. Here are some suggestions to keep your marriage growing and fresh.

Why not start by adding some spontaneity to your marriage relationship. Do the unexpected or unusual: Write your mate a letter and describe your first date and how you felt. If you send it to your mate's place of work, be sure to write "personal" on the envelope! If you take lots of slides, why not secretly put together a slide show of your marriage history? You could record a script on tape, with background music of "your song" from years past.

Consider kidnaping your mate for a couple of hours. Make reservations at a restaurant where you've never eaten and keep your destination a secret.

You could leave a love note in an unexpected place, taped to the toothpaste tube or folded in a pocket. Once you begin to think about it, you'll find all kinds of unusual and unexpected things you can do to keep your marriage fresh and flavorful.

As you surprise your mate and do the unexpected, watch out—you might get some surprises you're not expecting! One thing's for sure—your marriage won't stand still!

THE EMPTY NEST
IS COMING

How empty will your nest be when your children leave home? Now that's something we should all stop and think about. For some of us the empty nest is just ahead. What can we do to prepare for this new stage of life? Maybe your children are very young. The empty nest is far away, and you think this doesn't apply to you. Stop and think again. There are things you can do right now to make those empty nest years the best years of your married life.

We're in the process of emptying our nest with Jarrett and Joel away from home. In a very short time, Jonathan will also be gone. Actually we're in the stage called the wired nest—and have the telephone bills to prove it!

Wherever you are in your family life, you can do some things to prepare for those years when all the children leave home.

Here are some tips:

1. Look forward to growing old. Proverbs tells us that "Gray hair is a crown of splendor." With more years can come maturity of character.

2. Parenting is a temporary job, so don't let children crowd out intimacy.

3. Deal with problems as they arise. Problems don't go away. They'll still be with you in your empty nest if you don't deal with them now.

4. Develop interests and friends in common.

We agree that this coming stage might be the most fun stage of marriage. Your empty nest can be full if you're in it with your best friend!

MAIN COURSES

READING TOGETHER

Do you share ideas with your mate? If you're not quite sure, this might be an area to pursue.

Consider reading. How long has it been since you and your mate read a book or article and then discussed it? Reading together is one means of becoming closer intellectually.

A whole new area of intimacy in marriage can emerge when we start sharing thoughts and feelings generated by good literature. Here are some suggestions to get you started.

1. Try reading a book aloud together, perhaps at night before going to bed. It's a great way to relax.

2. You could try reading the same book privately. The husband underlines things of interest in red and the wife in blue. Then you could have a date and discuss your insights.

3. Ask what your mate is already reading. Then read the book or magazine yourself and discuss it.

4. Save newspaper and magazine articles of interest and share them.

It is possible to achieve intellectual closeness by reading together. To find the time, you may have to switch off the TV, delay the home-improvement project, or say no this week to band boosters, but your marriage will be better for it!

NINE

CHILD CENTERED OR COUPLE CENTERED?

Is your marriage couple centered or child centered? Being a parent in today's world is an awesome responsibility. It requires all the skills we can come up with, but are we practicing the skills for being a married person?

We know good marriages don't just happen. They require a lot of work and time investment too! While our challenge is to balance our roles of partner and parent, remember that the foundation for parenting is a strong commitment to your mate!

A child's most basic security is knowing that his parents love each other. Then the child is secure. He is a part of a strong, loving relationship and knows he will never be abandoned.

Recently we were planning a couple getaway. One of our sons remarked that it wasn't fair for us to go to the beach without him! We tried to assure him that it was for his own good. (We're not sure we convinced him.)

Do your children know that their parents really love each other? The greatest thing a dad can do for his child is to love the child's mom. And the greatest thing a mom can do for her child is to love the child's dad. Being a great partner will help you be a great parent.

BEING YOUR MATE'S BEST FRIEND

Is your mate your best friend? We hope so. Friendship is an important ingredient in marriage. Let's look at some elements of friendship that should be operating in a growing marriage.

Friendship means trusting, believing, and supporting one another. Can you trust each other? Does your mate know you believe in him or her? Do you give your mate the support needed?

Friendship requires time, and in order to grow, it must be cultivated. What are you doing today to cultivate a deeper friendship with your mate?

Why not make a list of things you'd like to do together to build your friendship. Include everything from an exotic evening out to washing the car together. Put the list somewhere where you can both see it, on the refrigerator or on the bathroom mirror.

As you spend time together, you'll become even better friends. There is nothing more relaxing than to feel completely comfortable with another person.

Wherever you are, you can start today cultivating a deeper friendship with your mate. Remember, a friend is somebody who knows you and likes you anyway!

ELEVEN

MARRIAGE SURVIVAL SKILLS

Did you realize that approximately one in every two marriages in the United States ends in divorce? The odds for survival aren't very encouraging.

How can we develop marriage survival skills? It would be great if the knowledge for a successful marriage could be issued along with the marriage license, but unfortunately that doesn't happen. Marriage skills are acquired skills—you have to spend some time learning them.

Actually, it can be a lot of fun. Psychologist and marriage expert Howard Markman says that preventive medicine is the smartest approach to marriage problems. Here are some of his tips for developing marriage survival skills that can help to prevent your marriage from becoming a statistic.

1. Keep your sense of humor. "Learn to laugh," he says. "Joy and laughter in a marriage is wonderful, healthful and smart."

2. Communicate daily.

3. Dream together and talk about your expectations. "Don't make the mistake," says Markman, "of thinking that your partner will know your needs and wants."

4. Learn how to resolve conflict, and remember to fight fairly. Stick to the issue when you're settling disagreements. Remember to attack the problem, not your mate!

5. Break the patterns of predictability. Don't let your routines turn into a rut.

Spend time together just by yourselves and examine your relationship. Start today to develop your marriage survival skills, and you won't become just another statistic.

TWELVE

NONVERBAL COMMUNICATION

Did you know you can say a lot without opening your mouth? It's quite possible to communicate without saying a word!

Recently at breakfast one of our sons said to Claudia, "Mom, stop nagging me." She replied, "I haven't said a word," and was told, "I know, Mom, but it's that nonverbal nagging!"

Did you realize that over half of our message is nonverbal? A Kodak Corporation research project showed that our nonverbal communication—the stares and glares—accounts for 58 percent of the total message.

Our tone of voice—the way we say things—makes up 35 percent of the message. We spend a lot of time thinking about the words we say, but the words are only 7 percent of the total message. Let's take a moment to think about the other things we do to communicate. Make a list of things you and your partner do to communicate without using words, like slamming doors, shrugging shoulders, or giving "the look." Write the nonverbal action in one column and what the action means in another column. Now check your list with one another and see if your interpretations are the same.

Another problem with communication arises when our nonverbal signals are different from our verbal message. There's nothing worse than to hear the right words, but underneath are hostility, bitterness, and a totally different message!

Nonverbal communication doesn't have to be negative. To top off this marriage-builder, think of five ways to say "I love you" without saying a word. Now get busy and use them!

THIRTEEN

TAKE AN ANNUAL
MARITAL CHECKUP

Is it time for an annual marital checkup? If you're thinking "What's a marital checkup?" then you are overdue! We advise every couple, no matter how long they've been married, to have an annual marital checkup. It can be the single most important thing you can do for your marriage.

Here's the good news. It doesn't have to cost a penny, and you don't need a marriage counselor or therapist to guide you. No stethoscopes or blood pressure cuffs are necessary. Just two pens, some paper, and a little uninterrupted time. It's guaranteed to bring back pleasant memories and accentuate the positive! Discuss the following questions:

1. What single thing delights me most about my mate?

2. What was the best thing that happened to me in the last twelve months?

3. What was the best thing that happened to us as a couple in the last twelve months?

4. If my mate had the power to change one thing about me, what do I think he or she would change?

5. Write down ten things you'd like to do together with your mate.

When you complete the questions, exchange answers with each other and enjoy reflecting on the last twelve months of your marriage. Combine your list of things you would like to do together, and set priorities. Pick a time and place to do your number one priority! During the next twelve months work your way through the list.

You may find this is the one annual checkup you'll actually look forward to. Go on and enjoy your marriage today!

HOW COMPATIBLE ARE YOU?

Compatibility is not a state in which you begin a marriage, but rather it's a goal to be achieved. Another way to look at matrimony and compatibility is: We fall in love with a personality, but we must live with a character. How have you changed since you were first married? Research reveals we become more compatible with our mates through learning to adapt to each other.

You can't change your basic personality, but you can change your behavior. In reviewing our marriage history, we realized we really have changed and adapted to each other over the years! What about you? Why not look back in your memory archives and see how you have changed and progressed toward compatibility. First, take two sheets of paper and each of you list all the ways you were similar when you first were married. You might think about your attitudes, your belief system, your interests, and your desires.

Second, write down the areas in which you were different—the areas you were less compatible. Third, think about which of your differences have given you the most trouble over the years. Have you made progress in resolving, or positively accepting, these differences? Fourth, what changes have you made in adapting to each other? Finally what reasonable changes do you still need to make? Take some time to share your lists with each other. Discuss how you have worked on your differences over the years. Have you grown and changed for the better in the process?

We found that while our similarities provided a foundation for our life together, real growth as persons has come mainly from working through our differences! You may discover the same is true in your marriage. The key is to remember that wherever you are now, you can keep adapting and moving closer to your mate. Remember, compatibility is not a state of being, but rather a goal to work for!

FIFTEEN

MAKING CONFLICT
WORK FOR YOU

Do you have an effective system for resolving conflict at your house? How can we make conflict work for us?

Psychologist David Mace states that the biggest problem in marriages today is not lack of communication. The biggest problem is the inability to deal with anger and conflict.

Let's look more closely at conflict and anger. How can we survive them and grow in our relationships? Good communication is important, but good communication is not enough. We need to consider four things.

First, conflict will be present, but it doesn't have to be destructive. Each conflict offers us a "growth point" or "choice point." To refuse to deal with conflict is to refuse growth in our relationship, and we don't want that.

Second, we need to realize that conflict can be painful. Anger that is released can cause pain, so we need to process our anger in the right way, like saying, "I'm angry," not "You make me so angry!"

Third, conflict can become overheated. Sometimes it's like a hot potato; we need to set it down and let it cool, or we'll get burned.

Fourth, to resolve a conflict after we've calmed down, we need to start the negotiations. Then we can logically consider the problem and create possible solutions.

Take a new look at conflict and anger. Turn them around and make them work for you. It's working at our house!

RESOLVING CONFLICT EFFECTIVELY

If you're married or in love, you know by experience that conflict does not signal a lack of love. The fact is—conflict is inevitable. Actually, conflict often means that love is very much alive and is attempting to break through some barrier that is separating you.

So the goal is not to avoid conflict, but to work through it. There's no substitute for periodically sitting down and airing issues and feelings with each other and honestly listening to each person's point of view.

In Chapter 15 you learned that the first step is to cool down. Now, after you've cooled down and can logically discuss the issue at hand, here are some helps we can give you.

Together write down these four steps and discuss each of them with your mate:

1. Define the problem. Go on and actually write out a summary of the issue at hand.

2. Identify who needs a solution and the other's contribution to the problem.

3. Suggest as many solutions as you can. Here it helps to brainstorm. Even write down the silly ones. If you can laugh together, it will help relieve the tension.

4. The last step is to select a plan of action you both can live with.

Remember, when you take the time to work through conflict, it can lead to better understanding and closer bonds of love. Try it, and you'll find conflict can be a friend instead of a foe at your house!

"HOW DO I LOVE THEE?"

How do I love thee? Let me count the ways." Perhaps Elizabeth Barrett Browning is one of your favorite poets too. This famous poet gives us a valuable lesson in how to build our marriage when she suggests that we count the ways we love each other. Let's take her good advice and look at some ways we can express our love to our mate.

Marriage specialist Dr. David Mace says that the healthiest families keep telling each other that they like each other.

Now you may not possess any poetic ability, but you can still count the ways you love your mate. Why not write them down and give them as a gift to your mate?

As you get started, think about these areas:

1. Character—What personality traits, moral strengths, and virtues do you appreciate?

2. Achievements—What about your mate's achievements?

3. Actions—What does your mate do for you that you appreciate?

4. Talents and Skills—What special abilities does your mate have?

Let us encourage you to write down what you appreciate. If you take Elizabeth Barrett Browning seriously, your marriage will be the better for it.

EIGHTEEN

STICK TO
ONE MODEL!

On his fiftieth wedding anniversary, Henry Ford was asked: "What is the formula for a good marriage?" He replied, "The same as for a successful car—stick to one model." If you haven't made it to your fiftieth anniversary yet, then we want to encourage you to take Henry Ford's advice and stick to one model.

It's important to have the attitude of permanence and commitment in a marriage relationship. It's vital to the stability of the marriage.

In the very near future, Dave's parents will be celebrating their fiftieth wedding anniversary. We're working on our twenty-seventh, but fifty years—now that's a long time! As we have observed their marriage, we've seen several important ingredients. One is commitment. For them divorce was never an option, so when problems came along, they had to work them out. The second thing we've observed is the importance of their relationship. They have worked at keeping close. They are soul mates and friends as well as lovers.

Some consider marriage a game—even a gamble. One person puts it this way: "Marriage is a gamble. You start with a pair. He shows a diamond. She shows a heart. Her father has a club. His father has a spade. There's usually a joker around somewhere, but after a while he becomes a king and she becomes a queen. Then they end up with a full house." We laugh, but let's remember, marriage is a permanent game. If you want to win, you can never throw in your hand! Why not affirm your commitment to your mate today!

PART THREE

TIME-FINDERS

DO YOU HAVE A FAST-LANE MARRIAGE?

Is your marriage stuck in the fast lane? You don't know how to slow it down? Fast-lane marriages are a modern trend and can be hazardous to your marital health. Sometimes it seems we're in the fast lane, making great time, but we're not sure where we're headed.

Just recently we picked up some hints that it's time to slow down. Do you, too, experience fast-lane stress?

Check these symptoms:

1. You have a list of topics to discuss but no time to discuss them.

2. You're going to bed later and getting up more tired.

3. You keep thinking things will slow down next week.

4. You make excuses about why you're too busy: "It's getting into my summer schedule. It's be-

cause of the swim meets. It will calm down after the music recital."

5.   You're more irritable and grouchy.

If you have noticed two or more of these symptoms, then maybe it's time to apply your brakes and slow your pace.

Sit down together for a cup of coffee and agree to reevaluate your activities. Ask yourself, "In light of eternity, how important is this activity?" Take the red pen to your schedule and be merciless!

Now choose a thirty-minute block of time that you can spend together with no agenda! Try it—this may help you overcome fast-lane stress at your house!

TWENTY

TIME FOR
MARRIAGE GOALS

In this hectic, fast-paced world, do you ever wish you had more time for each other? If we are honest, we would all probably have to say, "Yes." Let's do a little dreaming. Stop and think for a minute: "What things used to make our marriage fun and exciting?" What do you really desire for your marriage?

Write down both long- and short-range goals. Wayne Rickerson in his book, *We Never Have Time for Just Us*, gives these suggestions. Choose a few for yourselves.

- Plan a tradition, something you can do each year.

- Select another couple and begin to develop a friendship.

- Have dinner together, just the two of you, once a month.

- Schedule a yearly planning retreat for just the two of you.

- Dream about a trip to Hawaii or some other faraway, exotic place.

- Find one activity that can help you grow together when the children are gone.

- Set a regular time to walk and talk together.

- Pursue a hobby. Choose anything you want from rock hounding, mountain climbing, or photography to needlepoint. Take a class together or take up a sport together.

- Read a book together and discuss it.

- Once a year attend some type of marriage enrichment class, seminar, or retreat.

- Grow together spiritually by selecting a book on Christian living to study together—or attend a class and follow up with discussions just between the two of you.

- Share the Bible and pray together once a week.

- Start a savings account toward something you really want to do—even if it's only a dream!

Remember, dreams do come true! And in the process of your making them come true, your marriage will become more exciting and fun.

TWENTY-ONE

INCH BY INCH

Have you heard this saying—"Inch by inch life's a cinch, but yard by yard it's hard"? Do you feel overwhelmed by how far you have to grow in an area? We both experience that feeling from time to time.

Here's a good question. If life's a cinch by the inch, then why do we try to tackle things a yard at a time? We're not suggesting we should never set big and grandiose goals, but we are suggesting that we break our goals down into bite-size pieces.

For instance, if we want to lose fifteen pounds, we need to break that down into "inches." (We may want to lose those too!) We need to have a weekly goal—maybe for us that would be to lose one pound a week—or even one pound every two weeks. Now that's believable.

What about your marriage? Maybe the relationship is stale and boring. What would be an "inch" goal you could set? You can't change your whole situation overnight, but you can do something! Maybe you could plan a special evening together. Surprise your mate with an evening out at your favorite spot.

One "inch" we've been working on recently in our own relationship is to take a walk around the block each evening after dinner. It's fun to talk together without having to answer the phone. Maybe you want to take the initiative to sign up for the class you've been wanting to take together. Your "inch" is to call and register for the course.

Decide just how much your "inch" is, and start there. So mark this down and remember, yard by yard the job is hard, but inch by inch it's a cinch!

FINDING TIME
FOR EACH OTHER

The honeymoon is over when he phones that he'll be late for supper and she has already left a note that it's in the refrigerator. Sometimes it seems life gets too hectic and our marriage relationship gets the short end of the deal.

We all need to discover how to find time to keep our marriages alive and healthy. Good relationships don't just happen—they take work and effort. You'll find, though, it's really worth it!

Maybe you, like us, would like to add a few hours to each day. We can't do that, but we can use our time twice. Why not team up for some things that you usually have to do alone?

When we tackle the dishes together, it gives us a little extra time to talk. It's a safe time to talk about our boys—no one sticks around the kitchen when it's time to do the dishes!

Another place we can find some extra talking time is outside where all that yard work needs to be done! What about when you're going to a meeting or another activity? If you leave home a few minutes early or come home a little later, you can stop somewhere for a cup of coffee and a chat.

Maybe you'd like to plan a breakfast date and surprise your mate. You both may be surprised at how much time you can have together when you learn to use your time twice. Try it. It could be the time of your life!

KIDNAP
YOUR MATE

If your mate likes surprises, how about planning a getaway for two and kidnaping your mate? There was a kidnaping at our house several years ago and we still talk about it! Dave was looking for a special way to celebrate an anniversary and decided to surprise Claudia with two days away. What a surprise! Claudia found it hard to believe that Dave had taken care of all the details, such as a sitter for the boys, but he had.

Together we had a wonderful two days away. It was a special time we'll long remember. It was also special for our boys, since they helped in the planning.

Here are some tips to help you pull it off. If your budget is tight, consider using a friend's vacant apartment. Taking a picnic basket of goodies is cheaper than going to an expensive restaurant.

Kidnapings don't have to be overnight. A surprise evening can be exhilarating. If you can't arrange a whole evening, what about a surprise sixty-minute break for a cup of coffee, frozen yogurt, or diet cola!

Just taking the initiative and surprising your mate will mean a lot. Try it! We challenge you:

Add spice to your marriage and kidnap your mate. It'll be fun for you and your happy hostage!

THE LITTLE THINGS
ARE THE BIG THINGS

Think about this: In marriage the little things are really the big things! A good marriage must be built from little building blocks. Let's look at some of those big "little" things we can do to keep our marriages healthy.

Check and see how many you are using to build your marriage.

- Never being too old to hold hands.

- Remembering to say "I love you" at least once each day.

- Never going to sleep angry.

- Having the capacity to forgive.

- Having mutual objectives and values and standing together to face the world.

- Forming a circle of love that gathers the whole family.

- Speaking words of appreciation.

- Demonstrating gratitude in thoughtful ways.

- Giving each other an atmosphere in which each can grow.

- Looking together for the good side of things.

Remember, in a growing marriage the little things are the big things. It's not only marrying the right person. It's being the right partner. How are you doing with the little things in your marriage?

HAVING TROUBLE SAYING NO?

If you have trouble saying no, you have trouble! Let's look at the perils of overcommitment and how we can avoid them. We don't know about you, but we're both activists and it's hard to say no. We're learning. Just this week we were asked to take on another commitment—and we said, "Not this time."

When we get overcommitted we find ourselves fatigued and stressed. Fatigue and stress undermine even the strongest marriage.

It's hard to say no to people who need our services. People who are overcommitted continue to take more customers or clients, more committee work, more administrative responsibilities, more moonlights, more classes—you get the picture!

Overcommitment is an enemy of strong marriages. It's amazing that so many sensible and reasonable people become so involved with other activities that they become strangers to the people they love.

Stop and take a serious look at your lifestyle. Are you overcommitted? If the answer to that question is yes, decide to say no before the enemy, over-commitment, eliminates you. Believe it or not, this is one battle you can win!

BALANCING A
DUAL-CAREER MARRIAGE

Did you realize that husbands and wives are both employed outside the home in 50 percent of marriages? For whatever reason, there's a 50 percent chance you fall into the category of dual-career marriage.

If you're in this category, then you have an extra challenge. You may have a time and energy crisis. How can you team up for a growing marriage?

Here are some suggestions.

1. Listen to each other. It's important to talk about frustrations and successes. Make sure that you stay in touch by having a daily time when you regroup and share where you are.

2. Talk about what makes the household run smoothly. When you sit down together and communicate on this issue, you've won half the battle.

3. Work together. Remember, you're a team, and team members work together if they're going to win. So attack together the areas of responsibility like children, chores, and check writing.

4. Watch your social calendar, and remember to save time for just the two of you.

5. Here's one last tip. Concentrate on encouraging each other. We all need that.

Remember, working with your working mate may be your most rewarding job!

TWENTY-SEVEN

PARENT OR PARTNER?

Do your activities reflect your role as a partner or a parent? It's easy to get so involved in our kids' activities—soccer, football, band, or whatever—that we feel more like a chauffeur than a mate. How do we focus on our marriage in the middle of busy family schedules? We can start by evaluating our present activities.

Recently we were overloaded with work, and each of our boys had a heavy schedule of his own. As we checked out our schedules, it was obvious what was missing—time alone just for us.

We decided to take some time away from our hectic schedule. We couldn't afford to take it—no, we couldn't afford NOT to take it! Our date lasted several hours and helped us refocus on each other. When we returned home, we were much more productive. We were refocused on each other—not our immediate hassle!

Sometimes we find if we just take a fifteen-minute break with tall glasses of iced tea and focus on or touch base with each other, it helps. Life seems more manageable when we can step back—even if it's just for fifteen minutes!

Here's a tip for you. Your children's activities are important, but don't allow yourself to become a slave to your parenting role and forget your partner! So, parents, take some time right now to refocus on your partner. Your marriage will be stronger for it!

PART FOUR

MARRIAGE VITAMINS

TWENTY-EIGHT

MARRIAGE VITAMINS

Why not add that extra touch of health to your marriage by giving each other marital vitamins? A marriage vitamin is any thing we do to build up our mate.

One clever husband took this suggestion literally and bought thirty empty capsules. He then typed out thirty compliments for his wife and put one in each capsule. On the bottle he wrote, "Take one a day for encouragement."

We really do need daily encouragement from our mates. It's got to start somewhere, so why not with you? Take a couple of minutes right now to make a list of ways you can build up and encourage your mate.

You could start with a phone call to say, "Hi, honey, I just wanted to call and say I love you and appreciate you!" We all like to get phone calls like that!

Use your own creativity, but let us give you this warning—marriage vitamins are habit forming, but they can be very beneficial to your marital health!

TWENTY-NINE

DO YOU HAVE A MARRIAGE ROAD MAP?

When we start on a trip, one thing we always take along is a road map. It helps us get to our destination without too many problems. Marriage is similar. We need to know where we are going in our relationship. We need a marriage road map. Here's a question for you. Do you know where your marriage is headed and how to get there?

Before a map can be useful, you have to identify where you are on the map. Then you can progress to where you want to be. Here are a couple of questions that will help you see where you are in your marriage.

1. Do you have goals in your marriage? Goals on a marriage map are like cities along the way on a travel map. Goals give us a direction in which to head.

2. Do you have common goals? There's a real problem if one wants to go to Miami and the

other wants to head for New York. Marriage goals need to be mutual to be useful.

3. You'll never have common goals unless you can answer yes to this next question: "Have you talked about your goals with each other?" If you haven't, then here is a starting place in making your marriage map.

Here's an action point for you. List some goals for your marriage.

You might consider short-term goals. What would you like to see happen in your marriage in the next six months? Maybe you've been wanting to date weekly. That could go under short-term goals.

Don't overlook listing some long-term goals too. Think about where you want to be in your marriage in five, ten, or twenty years! Trust us; mapping out your marriage can result in a trip you will enjoy!

THIRTY

RECHARGING YOUR MARITAL BATTERIES

Do your marital batteries need recharging? From time to time we realize our batteries are low on juice. We need to do something to recharge them. For us, recharging our marital batteries always involves time alone with one another. Family vacations are a must; they're important for building family relationships and memories. But we think mates need just-for-two vacations as well.

Marriage therapists tell us we need time alone. We live such responsible lives that we sometimes need to get away. They suggest taking off our watches and being completely irresponsible once in a while, doing whatever strikes our fancy, sleeping till noon or having breakfast at two A.M. or P.M.

You may be thinking, "It's just impossible. We don't have the time or the money." Vacations don't have to be long or expensive—they just have to be! If you're serious about it, you'll find a way.

Perhaps you could swap children with another family for the weekend. Whatever you have to do, it's worth it.

What happens when we take a vacation, even if it is for only twenty-four hours? We break the humdrum monotony of the dailies. We leave our troubles and problems behind, and we refocus on each other. We challenge you to look at your schedule for the next few weeks and carve out some time. Vacations for two are worth all the hassle and work to pull them off. Plus you'll recharge your batteries!

MIND READING

"People who have lived together for a long time can read each other's minds." Would you say this statement is true or false? It's true that after twenty-six years of marriage we can often predict what the other will do or say, but that's far from being a mind reader.

So let us dispense with the myth that partners can read each other's minds. If we assume we can read each other's minds, we pave the way for misunderstanding. Since we all continue to grow and change throughout life, only we know what we're thinking.

Here's an action point for you: Really listen to each other today. Don't assume you know what the other is thinking. Even at times when we aren't mind reading, we may miss the real message. The next time you're not sure you understand what your mate is saying, you could say something like, "Honey, this is what I heard you saying. . . . Am I right?" This gives the other person the chance to confirm that you've got it right or to clarify the meaning.

So next time resist the urge to tell your mate what he or she is thinking. Remember, most of us are poor mind readers. Besides, it's more fun to listen, to ask questions, and to talk with one another.

TEACHING OLD DOGS
NEW TRICKS

You can teach an old dog new tricks! We used to think we couldn't teach old dogs new tricks, but a recent study of the aged shows that we can change our behavior until the day we die. We are never too old to learn!

It's nice to know we don't just have to put up with each other. We can grow in our relationship and continue to adapt to one another.

We would have a pretty boring marriage if we stopped growing and adapting to each other. We can't change our basic personalities, but we can modify our behavior.

One key to change is to be willing to change. We may have a tendency to be late, but if we want to change in this area, research says we can.

How about you? Have you learned any new tricks lately? Is there an area in which you need to change? Remember, it's never too late to make a change for the better.

It's good to know that a commitment to growth will keep your marriage healthy—until the day you die. And that's the dog-gone truth!

FORGIVENESS—SAYING YOU'RE SORRY

The need for forgiveness is universal. No two people agree on everything, and if they did, one would be unnecessary. Unfortunately when we don't see eye to eye, we often become irritated with each other and say things we later regret. When we do, we need to clear the air and forgive one another.

A relationship must include forgiveness if it is to grow. In the closeness of a marriage, we have lots of opportunities to forgive and ask for forgiveness.

Maybe you find yourself needing to ask for forgiveness from time to time. Maybe you're in that situation right now. Stop and ask yourself:

1. Have I used any unkind words lately?

2. Have I broken my mate's trust?

3. Have I selfishly ridden over the rights of others?

4. Have I allowed bitterness and hate to enter my life? Nothing kills a relationship more quickly than bitterness, hate, or resentment.

Now is the time to clear the air. Ask your mate for forgiveness today.

Remember to do it in the right way. Start your sentence with "I" and let the statement reflect back on you. You could say something like, "I'm sorry I was angry and shouted at you. Will you please forgive me."

Don't say, "You made me so angry. Of course, anyone would shout about what you did, but would you forgive me anyway?" How you ask for forgiveness can make a big difference in your mate's response. Remember! Let the statement reflect back on you.

Forgiveness is vital to healthy relationships. It's the oil that lubricates the friction of closeness in the daily routine of a marriage!

THIRTY-FOUR

DOES YOUR MONEY END BEFORE THE END OF THE MONTH?

Does your money run out before the end of the month? Most of us have to answer yes to that question from time to time. When your finances are chronically snarled, you may be suffering from some unhealthy attitudes. If so, there's no time like the present to make some changes, in both your attitudes and your behavior. We work continuously to control our finances instead of having our finances control us. What can we do to stretch our finances to reach the end of the month?

Here are three principles that are helping us.

1. Don't depend on tomorrow. Do you want to buy something you know that you'll have the money to pay for next week? It's hard, but we are trying to learn to wait until next week. None of us knows what tomorrow may bring. You may get a raise, but you may lose your job!

2. Second, if you don't have any money to spend, stay away from the stores. If you and

your little plastic cards aren't in the store, you won't be tempted by all those bargains. Now if we could learn that one principle! When you think about it, it's smart just to stay away. Window shopping when your cash flow is low makes as much sense as hanging around a bakery when you're on a diet.

3. Third, separate need from greed. Before buying anything, ask yourself, "Do I really need this? If I buy it will I be straining my budget?" Always step back from possible purchases and look at them in the light of common sense and reason. If you question the purchase, that might be a signal to wait.

Apply these three principles, and think how great it will be to enjoy the end of the month! There's no time like now to make some changes.

THIRTY-FIVE

ENRICHING IN-LAW RELATIONSHIPS

When you married your spouse, did you accept your spouse's parents as well? Judging from all the in-law jokes, in-law relations may be the most neglected and abused of all family relationships. How can you build healthy relationships with your in-laws? The more mutual respect and enjoyment you experience with your mate's parents, the more security and stability you and your spouse will feel in your marriage.

If you'd like to maintain a growing friendship with your in-laws, here are some ideas you may want to try:

1. Write a letter to your partner's parents thanking them for a character trait or personal skill they instilled in your mate.

2. The next time you visit your in-laws' home, look for something you can do for them.

Maybe you could run an errand or help in the kitchen or yard. Look for some way to serve them.

3. Keep grandparents informed of your children's activities, interests, and accomplishments. Grandparents especially love newspaper clippings and lots and lots of pictures. Every couple of years we make sure our parents have an updated picture of the Arp clan.

4. If you live a long distance apart and don't see them frequently, schedule a regular visit by phone. The cost will be low compared to the rewards.

Above all, be grateful to your in-laws. They were the ones who provided the climate for cultivating all the attractive qualities in that special person you chose to marry! Remember, in making family ties stronger, you'll make your marriage stronger as well!

DISCUSSION STARTERS

TAKING AN IMAGINARY TRIP

Do you feel as close to your mate as you did before marriage? Maybe you don't feel as close as you once did, and you're not sure who moved or how it happened. But you do want to start moving closer.

To help you do this, let us take you on an imaginary trip. Close your eyes and think back into your past. . . .

Can you remember the first time you ever saw your mate?

What do you remember about your first date? Where did you go? How did you feel?

Think back to when you first realized that you really cared for each other and the relationship was going somewhere.

Do you remember the first time you ever talked about getting married?

Now think about your wedding day.

What do you recall about that first place you called home? When we were first married, we lived in a tiny terrace apartment. We had to walk up two steps to the bathroom, but the ceiling was the same height as in the rest of the apartment. It was fortunate that neither of us is tall because our bathroom ceiling was about six feet high.

Maybe you, like us, were as poor as church mice and decorated your abode in what we called early marriage. All hand-me-down furniture was accepted. We'll never forget our hand-me-down bed. The slats were too short and our bed kept falling in.

Here's an action point for you. Have a date with your mate and share memories from your dating days and your first months of marriage. Good memories build good marriages. Besides it's just plain fun!

NEEDED — MORE AFFIRMATION

If people are to grow into what they can be, they need to be appreciated for what they are. Here's a tip for you—give your mate a gift of affirmation.

How long has it been since you gave your mate a sincere compliment? Unfortunately, we all need reminders. We aren't really encouraged to affirm each other. In the world today it's often considered chic to be casually critical of others. "Put-downs" are used as a form of friendly conversation.

Sometimes we find it easy to exchange insulting familiarities, but difficult to express approval and admiration. It's even more difficult to receive praise from others. So we want to offer you an exercise that can be a gift of affirmation for both you and your mate. Sit down with your spouse and write ten things you really like about one another. Now, that's not so hard to do.

Then move on to the second part, which may be a little harder. Write ten things you really like about yourself. Go ahead, and don't be intimidated by false modesty. List your good qualities—at least ten of them.

Now share your lists. Do you have any uncomfortable feelings? Admit them. They'll disappear quickly as you give each other this gift of affirmation. Do it. You're worth it!

THIRTY - EIGHT

ARE YOU GOOD ROLE MODELS?

What's in store for your children if they pattern their marriages after yours? Now that's something to think about! Whether we realize it or not, we are being a marriage role model. It's sobering to think that right now we are influencing marriages of the future—our children's marriages.

When your children are grown and ready to marry, how do you think they'll be influenced by the example you've set for them? Check the following areas and rate yourself good, average, or poor.

1. We have clear and honest communication.

2. We do a good job of managing and processing our anger.

3. We're able to resolve disagreements.

4. We express affection and love to one another.

5. We're companions and friends.

6. We work together as a team.

7. We demonstrate understanding.

8. We are able to forgive and change when needed.

9. We have similar spiritual values.

Why not take time with your mate and talk over how you're doing in these areas? Remember, in building your marriage, you're influencing the future marriages of your children!

MARRIAGE IS THE BEGINNING

Is marriage the beginning or the end? Often marriage is portrayed as the end of the story. Many books, movies, and plays end when the ideal couple meet, fall in love, are married, and ride off into the sunset.

Happy ending or unrealistic beginning? After marriage, we tend to relax. We don't work as hard on our relationship as we did before marriage.

And relationships don't remain static—they're either growing or regressing. What can you do today to help your marriage be on the growing edge?

Why not think back and then for twenty-four hours pretend you're still dating. Write a love note or buy a small gift for your sweetheart—just because you're obsessed with thoughts of your mate!

Recently we sat up really late to watch the late show. Would you like to know why two sensible middle-aged people would do that?

We'll tell you—this middle-aged husband and wife are confirmed romantics, and the movie on the late, late show was the same movie we went to see on our first date twenty-eight years ago.

Perhaps you have an old scrapbook you could pull out. We still have one that boasts one dried-out poison oak leaf Dave gave to Claudia as a souvenir. Doesn't that make you itch? We did! That's one memory we suggest you don't ever touch!

Get busy today and see what excitement you can add to your marriage. Remember—the rest of the story is the beginning of the story—not the end!

FORTY

SEPARATENESS AND TOGETHERNESS

Is it possible to be too close to your mate? Some couples complain of not having enough time with each other. On the other end of the spectrum are the couples who are together continuously. The question is, "How can we reach the right balance?" Take us, for example. We work closely together, but we've found that too much togetherness can be negative. At times we simply need a break from each other.

The opposite is the couple whose lives and activities barely ever cross paths. We know one couple who both travel in their jobs. Their communication time is at 11 P.M. when the phone rates go down!

Somewhere there is a balance. To see where you are in this area, make a list of your different responsibilities and activities.

Then go back and label them as:

- A: Something I do mainly alone.

- T: Something I do mainly with my mate.

- O: Something I do mainly with people other than my mate.

Take some time and discuss your list with one another. Then discuss the following three questions:

1. Are we doing enough creative things together to build our relationship?

2. Are we involved in enough activities to meet our separate needs as individuals?

3. Do we need to make any changes in our activities in order to keep a healthy balance?

If the answer to that last question is yes, it's time to pull out your calendar and make some changes! Remember, it will add to the balance sheet of your marriage!

FORTY-ONE

TILL DEBT
DO US PART

Have you heard the saying, "Till debt do us part"? Perhaps this is a sensitive subject in your home. If so, it's time to discuss finances and how they relate to the marriage team. Money and its management are a sore spot in many relationships. Often we come into marriage with different viewpoints on and styles of managing money.

Whether you have little or much, the key issues are whether you can communicate about finances and whether you are pulling together for solutions or pushing apart.

To see if you are a team in this area of your marriage, answer together these four questions.

1. Have you had a disagreement or felt tension in your relationship about finances in the last month?

2. Is friction caused by differences in your backgrounds? Maybe one of you grew up in a family who watched every penny, and the other grew up thinking money grew on trees.

3. Have you had good training and experience in managing money? The mate who said, "Honey, I can't be overdrawn. I still have ten checks left!" needs to learn more about banking.

4. What happens when money is really tight? When we are under tremendous financial pressure, we have to be especially committed to pulling together.

How about you? Perhaps a starting place is to sit down and look at your finances together and discuss these four questions. Remember, if you pull together, your finances won't push you apart.

FORTY-TWO

CHANGING TO
REMAIN THE SAME

About the only constant thing about life is change. A new job or a new baby might mean a totally different routine, so we have to adjust our schedules to maintain positive relationships. We change in order to remain the same.

Change is something we can't escape nor should we want to. It's all around us, and it does affect our family and our marriage. Sometimes it may become necessary for us to change in order to remain the same.

Our life is changing now as our boys get older. Joel and Jarrett have both left the nest and Jonathan will only be with us for a short time. It seems only yesterday that we were in the diaper stage, and now we're approaching the empty nest.

Wherever you are in your life, you're probably also experiencing changes in some area. What are the changes in your life right now? Maybe it's a move, a new job, or a new baby. How do you handle change in your relationship?

Here are some tips that will help you adjust to the changes in your life.

- Realize that change and growth in marriage and family life are healthy. Many times difficult situations and changes actually strengthen our relationship.

- Revise your expectations. Don't expect life to remain the same.

- Don't sacrifice growth for stability in your family relationship. If the boat is never rocked, it never goes anywhere! Coexistence is not growth. Make sure you're staying in touch with one another as the family changes.

- Be willing to try new things. Make a mid-course correction if needed. Remember, even a small change in direction can make a major difference in where you're headed!

PART SIX

DIVORCE PROOFERS

BEATING THE ENEMY—BOREDOM

How would you like to divorce-proof your marriage? The tips we have given you should help you to fill that tall order. But the worst enemy of marriage could be just plain boredom. Are you in a marriage *rut*?

Sameness in marriage is like zucchini squash eaten ten days in a row. We have a vegetable garden, and we can grow zucchini really well. The first servings of zucchini are delicious, but as the days go by, we begin to overdose on it. Once Claudia even made zucchini cookies, which was fine until Jonathan noticed the green specks!

Are you on a marriage diet of the same old thing? Don't panic if you are—there is real hope! Here's an action point to get you out of your marriage rut.

1. First, start dating. Yes, that is what you did before you were married! Make a list of fun ideas and choose one a week. Once we asked other

couples to tell us their favorite dates. Here are some of the things they shared.

- fly kites in an open field
- picnic in the mountains
- visit the zoo without the children
- go on a hike
- camp out overnight
- go to the symphony

2. Second, change the routine—do the unusual. Bring your mate a cup of coffee in bed or make love in a new or unusual place or take a walk in the rain or eat breakfast in the dining room.

Your friends may think you're crazy, but we promise you, you'll beat the enemy—boredom!

FORTY-FOUR

AVOIDING EMOTIONAL DIVORCE

Would you like to avoid "emotional divorce" in your marriage? Who wouldn't say "Yes" to a question like that? All too often couples start out with good communication and intimacy, but somewhere along the way they lose it.

Charles Sell, in his book, *Achieving the Impossible: Intimate Marriage,* offers some great suggestions. One important factor is learning to deal with our own negative feelings. Face it—we all have them at times. When we do, we need to admit that we have them.

Repressing negative emotions is a natural reaction, but it's also similar to collecting saving stamps. Sooner or later, the book fills up, and we turn it in for payment.

Admitting our feelings, however, is only the beginning. Next, we learn to process them. Here are four steps for doing just that.

1. Learn to forgive. This has to be the first step. To make it easier, remember the times you were the one who needed to be forgiven. No one is perfect, and from time to time we all blow it. Go on and forgive your mate when the time rolls around.

2. Get some exercise. We've found that physical exertion can substitute for destructive ways of venting anger. Maybe you like to work in the garden or jog or get out and hit some tennis balls. Whatever you do, it will give you a chance to vent your anger and maintain some composure as you try to work on a genuine solution.

3. Use words to explain how you feel. Too often we communicate, but not with words. Instead we send a message through nonverbal gestures like icy silences, slamming doors, or facial expressions. We all can recognize "The Look"! It's much better to use words and say how we're feeling.

4. The last step really goes along with the third one. Cool down before you speak. You can say "I'm angry," but you may need to stop there until you're more in control of yourself. Some situations are like hot potatoes—you need to let things cool down or you'll get burned!

Here is one final thought. Remember, attack the problem and not your mate, and you'll avoid emotional divorce at your house!

FORTY-FIVE

SECRETS OF A HAPPY MARRIAGE

Modern marriages last an average of 9.4 years—considerably less than forever. Too often the "I do" dissolves into "I don't, I can't, and I won't." Yet for every marriage that crumbles, another endures. What are some of the key ingredients in those good marriages that endure?

Some people think the keys for an enduring marriage are sex and romantic lives. They are wrong. "Love is a prerequisite to launching a good marriage, but it isn't enough to keep the marriage afloat," says psychologist Howard Markman.

More important than how much two people love each other, or how happy they are before the wedding, is how well they talk and share and work out their problems after marriage.

In other words, how they deal with their feelings matters more than what they're actually feeling. Here are ten common characteristics of happy couples. Check and see how many describe your marriage!

1.   They're best friends.

2.   They listen to and confide in each other.

3.   They're tuned in to each other's feelings.

4.   They can deal with negative emotions.

5.   They know how to handle conflict.

6.   They're less than brutally honest. In other words, they think before they talk.

7.   They trust each other.

8.   They're committed to making the marriage work.

9.   They share interests.

10.   They're flexible enough to change and tolerate change.

The good news from the marriage researchers is that couples learn how to be happily married. It's possible, they say, to master the skills needed to make your relationship better. And that's good news!

FORTY-SIX

WINDOWS AND WALLS

Are you building windows or walls in your marriage? How are you doing on cultivating transparency with your mate? A real relationship includes letting one another see what's in our hearts—what's happening on the inside. We believe we can build this kind of openness. We can keep the walls torn down and the windows of communication wide open.

The people we're comfortable with are usually those who reveal themselves to us. Why, then, do we often choose to build walls? Maybe we want to appear tough, self-reliant, and macho, or maybe we build walls because we're afraid of rejection. Whatever the reason for building walls, we need to eliminate them and get the windows open.

To help get you started, we challenge you to share one inner feeling with your mate today. Remember, start with a positive one! Start your statement with "I" and let it reflect back on you. Here are two examples: "I feel so good and secure when you express your love to me" or "I really feel part of your life when you share what's happening at work with me."

To help your mate open a window, you might follow with, "Now tell me how you feel." You'll find opening windows can be refreshing at your house.

FORTY-SEVEN

YOU'RE NOT LISTENING!

Have you ever been accused of not listening? As hard as we try to listen, we're afraid that at times we're both guilty of not listening. Not listening plays a big part in problem marriages. Counselors hear over and over again statements like "He never listens to me" or "She doesn't understand how I feel."

If poor listening is a sign of a troubled marriage, then good listening is a characteristic of a healthy marriage. When others listen to us, we feel important, understood, and accepted.

Good listening can improve a relationship. Here's an action point for you. Determine today to improve your listening score. Remember these tips.

1. Empathize; don't criticize. Unsolicited advice may be criticism!

2. Give your mate full attention when he or she is talking. Often when our mate is talking, we're either thinking about what we're going to say next or we're paying attention to something else, like preparing dinner or watching TV.

3. Listen for feelings, but don't judge them. They are simply how your mate feels. That's valuable information for you.

4. Don't interrupt. You'll get your turn. You can listen best with your mouth closed.

Remember, practice makes perfect. Plan the time in your schedule today to talk with and listen to your mate. You may be surprised at what you hear!

FORTY-EIGHT

MIDDLE-AGED MARRIAGE

Do you have a middle-aged marriage? Somewhere between thirty and sixty we begin to see ourselves as middle-aged. Marriages, also, may be perceived as middle-aged. What about yours?

The middle years of a marriage start when the children begin to leave the nest and end when spouses leave their jobs. It's often a time when partners must change and adapt to keep their relationship satisfying. When you're at this stage or close to it, you may recognize some shifts in your responsibilities, interests, and concerns.

One nice thing is that you and your mate may have more time to talk together, do things together, and make plans for the future. You may even have more time to express your love and appreciation.

We are just getting into this stage of marriage with two of our sons gone and the last one leaving home soon. We're finding it may be the best stage of family life yet.

It's a good time to reflect on our experiences together, to look at how our relationship has grown and changed over the years, and to reaffirm those things we really value about our marriage.

Wherever you are in your marriage, middle age or just married, take some time to look at your relationship. Here are some questions to get you started.

1.   What personal traits are special to you about your mate?

2.   What has your partner done that you especially like?

3.   What do you particularly enjoy doing together?

4.   What do you appreciate now, more than ever before?

Discuss these questions together. Your partner's comments may help you see your marriage in a different light. Remember, marriages thrive when partners give each other time. Stop and take time for your marriage today. It's a lifetime investment you can't afford not to make!

FORTY-NINE

GIVING A GIFT
OF TIME

The most important gifts can't be bought or even gift-wrapped in a box. The most meaningful gifts may cost a lot—but not in dollars and cents!

Are you searching for an extra special gift for that person you love? Perhaps you're looking for some creative ideas. Here are a few we've found to help you get started:

1. Give coupons instead of the usual presents.

Each coupon is good for certain activities or things you know your partner would appreciate:

- a day off while you baby-sit

- a promise to limit TV viewing to one hour each day

- a special meal out

- an evening to fill as you please!

2. Write a letter or compose a poem to express your love.

3. Put together a photo album of special times together. Be sure to include some pictures from your dating days.

4. Write a marriage history of your high times together.

Think about this: The best gift doesn't have to cost money. It's a gift of ourselves.

FIFTY

FIVE MINUTES
TO TALK

If you discovered you only had five minutes to talk, what would you say? Too often we take each other for granted and assume we will always be there. We often go through our busy days leaving much unsaid that we would really like to say. If people discovered that they had only five minutes to say all they wanted to say, every telephone booth would be occupied by people calling other people to tell them once again that they loved them. Why wait until the last five minutes?

Here is an action point for you. Why not take a few minutes alone to reflect on what you would say to your mate if you only had five minutes. You might think about his or her character qualities, skills, or talents, or think about special things your mate does for you.

Write these things down. There are several things you can do with your list. Put it in the form of a letter or poem, and put it under a pillow or mail it to your mate. If you mail it to the office, be sure to write "personal" on the outside!

You may want to keep your list and give your mate one honest compliment each day for the next few weeks. It may become a habit you'll want to keep. Let us warn you! Be prepared for a better relationship with your mate. So why wait for the last five minutes when you can enrich your marriage today!

MINI-MOMENTS

FIFTY ONE

ARE YOU A GIVER
OR A TAKER?

Are you a giver or a taker in your marriage? If we're really honest, we'd have to say both! But for now, let's consider how to be a giver in the marriage relationship. One husband said, "We have a lot of give and take in our relationship—I give and my wife takes!" Now that's not what we're talking about. Neither are we talking about the philosophy, "You scratch my back, and I'll scratch yours."

How much better to have a giving marriage. When God said it is more blessed to give than receive, He knew what He was talking about.

Stop and think, What can you give to your marriage today? As one person put it: The more you give, the more you get. / The more you love, the less you fret. / The more you do unselfishly, / The more you live abundantly. / The more of everything you share, / The more you'll always have to spare. / The more you love, the more you'll find / That life is good and friends are kind, / For only what we give away / Enriches us from day to day.

Stop for a minute and reflect on what you can give to your marriage today. Is there something your mate wants you to do? Then do it! Go ahead and enrich your marriage today—be a giver instead of a taker!

FIFTY-TWO

HAVE YOU HUGGED
YOUR PARTNER TODAY?

Have you given your honey a hug today? We can't overemphasize the importance of touch in the marriage relationship. Hugs are an important part of life at our household. How about at your house?

We all need to be touched. Newborn babies can actually die from the absence of touching. Our need to be touched persists all our lives; touch is almost as essential as food.

Let's look at what a hug can communicate:

- It can say, "You're appreciated; you're okay; I care about you."

- It can relieve stress.

- It can heal old wounds.

- It can comfort more than words.

Hugs help to fill our emotional tank. If your emotional tank is empty, why not put a sign up in a prominent place that says, "I need a hug." And remember, when you give a big hug, you get one back at the same time.

Here's your action point. Hug someone you love today, and for the next week give that person a minimum of three hugs a day.

Remember, a hug restores the soul—and the relationship!

TWENTY-FIVE CENTS WILL CHANGE YOUR MATE'S DAY

There are still a few bargains around. A twenty-five-cent phone call is one of them! It's a great way to enrich your marriage. Go ahead and call your mate today. Tell your mate that you care, that he or she is special and that you love him or her. It may be the best investment you ever make, and you'll reap the benefits. So reach out and touch someone—specifically your mate!

If you call from your home or office, the call will probably be free, but if you must use a pay phone, go ahead and invest twenty-five cents in your marriage.

Take advantage of answering machines if you happen to have one. You can leave all kinds of personal messages. But take our advice and listen to your messages alone. Dave has a couple of friends who still don't believe the message they overheard was actually from Claudia!

Why not make the phone work for you and enrich your marriage? Everyone likes a bargain,

and here is one that is available daily, the telephone!

FIFTY-FOUR

CLEARING
THE AIR

There is one key activity that will help to keep your marriage healthy, vital, and strong. This key to an alive marriage is to resolve small conflicts as they come up. Resolving these conflicts will remove hostility and bitterness, restore the flow of love, facilitate forgiveness, and help us to continue to affirm each other.

We really do need to deal with the small things that come up. When we do that, we clear the air. We open up the communication that was temporarily blocked. We improve all the aspects of our marriage.

Dealing with small conflicts is good for the relationship just as exercising is good for the body. It's a kind of marital jogging. It clears the head and makes it possible to think clearly about other things as well.

Here's an action point for you. Is there some little area that's causing conflict in your relationship with your mate? Now's the time to clear the air.

You can bring a breath of fresh air to your marriage! Think about that!

SAYING
"I LOVE YOU"

When was the last time you said "I love you" to your mate? If you can't remember, it's been much too long! If you can remember and it's been in the last twenty-four hours, you get a big fat A+.

If you've said "I love you" to your spouse more than twenty-four hours ago and less than a week ago, give yourself a B. Not bad, but you could do a little better.

Now if you can remember saying "I love you," but it's been over a week, you get a C for remembering. If you can't remember the last time you spoke those words, you flunk, and improvement is needed.

Here's a follow-up question: Does your mate from time to time have to ask, "Do you love me?" If so, it's been too long since you've used those three important words, "I love you."

Now here's the good news. You may have failed, but don't get discouraged. You can raise your grade to an A+ just as quickly as you can pick up the phone, call your mate, and say, "Honey, I love you!" Or raise your score by sending your mate a letter, card, or telegram to say, "I love you."

Don't worry about overdoing it. You can't say a sincere "I love you" too often. Try it. You'll see what we mean!

COMPLETING THE COMMUNICATION CYCLE

How can I tell if what I heard is what you said? Good communication is at the core of any healthy relationship.

Words mean many different things. Sometimes our messages get muddled. We mean to convey one message, but our mate hears something completely different. This can lead to all kinds of misunderstandings, and misunderstandings disrupt family unity. What can we do to insure that what I hear is what you said?

Here's one method to make sure the other person is hearing what we really said and meant. Check out what you hear by saying to your mate, "This is what I heard you saying—is that what you meant?"

You're not saying you agree; you're simply asking if you're getting the message straight. Then your mate can confirm that you heard correctly. If not, your mate can try to get the message across again.

It's a good feeling to know your mate understands or wants to understand. So today try completing the communication cycle at your house.

First, one person makes a statement.

Second, the other person gives feedback. "This is what I hear you saying. Is that what you meant?"

Third, the first person confirms or corrects the message. Keep talking until you both agree that what is being said is the same message that is being heard. Remember, a rewarding part of marriage and family life is being understood!

FIFTY - SEVEN

CHOOSE A
TLC SIGN

What do you do when you need tender loving care? Do you have a signal you can give to your mate when you're in desperate need for a little TLC? You can choose a signal.

An old farm couple we heard about learned how to signal each other when they needed extra encouragement. If the husband needed TLC, he'd walk into the kitchen and throw his hat down on the table. This was his signal that he needed his wife to encourage him.

Similarly, if he discovered that his wife was wearing her apron backward, he knew she needed him to help her bear her burdens. We've been known to launch a media campaign to let each other know we need hugs and a little attention. Right now there's a sign on our refrigerator that says, "I need a hug!"

Signs are fine, but if they're ignored, then speak up and tell someone that you need some attention and love.

What could you do to let each other know you need some TLC? Why not sit down together and choose a signal that will alert the other to your special need? You could touch your nose with your hand or stand on one foot or anything as long as your mate knows beforehand what it means.

Try it today. Developing your own TLC signals can help you to build a habit of encouragement!

FIFTY - EIGHT

"OUCH, I FELT A PINCH!"

How do you handle the little "pinches" in your marriage? You know, those times you would like to say "Ouch!" We call those little hurts pinches. Have you ever felt any at your house?

What's a pinch? It's what you feel when your mate says something that gives a little hurt. It's no big deal, but it doesn't feel good.

How can we handle pinches? In our marriage we simply say, "Ouch, I felt a pinch!" This alerts the other to our feelings, and we can clear the air right then.

We have also used the pinch concept with our boys. Try it with your mate and children, but first be sure to explain what a pinch is.

Along the same line, you can give a thumbs up signal for "Keep talking, you're coming through loud and clear." Thumbs down means, "You're treading on thin ice!"

Try our tips, or come up with your own signals. We promise you that it'll help you to deal with little hurts and to refrain from being a pincher in your family!

FIFTY NINE

WANT SOME WARM FUZZIES?

Why not be original and give your mate some warm fuzzies? Just what is a warm fuzzy?

It's that feeling you get when someone you love does something to let you know you're special. It's a warm fuzzy feeling. Why not share that feeling with your mate today? Give your spouse an envelope of warm fuzzies.

Here's how. Simply write on small pieces of paper some things you think your mate would enjoy:

- One big bear hug

- A sixty-second passionate kiss

- A coupon good for one back rub or for a candlelight bubble bath for two or, if you're more conservative, for a walk around the block—holding hands

Now fold each piece, put them in an envelope, and label it "Warm Fuzzies for My Lover." Let your mate open them one by one.

It may be cold outside, but this is one way your mate can feel warm, loved, and fuzzy!

DO YOUR MARRIAGE
A FAVOR—JOIN ACME

An international network of persons working for better marriages, the Association of Couples in Marriage Enrichment (ACME), was established in 1973 by David and Vera Mace. There are now more than 4,600 members in thirty-two countries who have joined together in this work. How does ACME help couples? Activities focus on prevention, growth, and potential. Couples learn to communicate effectively, to deal creatively with anger, to negotiate differences, and to express appreciation. Through weekend retreats, local marriage growth groups, conferences, and a practical monthly newsletter, you'll have the opportunity to continue to enrich your marriage relationship. ACME activities are for couples of all ages and in every stage of marriage. So whether your are a pre-married, newlywed, remarried, two-career couple, middle-aged couple, retiree—whatever your situation, let us encourage you to consider becoming a member of the Association of

Couples in Marriage Enrichment. You'll experience new growth in your marriage.

For more information or to join ACME, write to:

THE ASSOCIATION FOR COUPLES
IN MARRIAGE ENRICHMENT
502 N. Broad St.
P.O. Box 10596
Winston-Salem, NC 27108

The telephone number is 919-724-1526 or 800-634-8325. The membership fee is modest and is a great investment!

BIBLIOGRAPHY

Arp, Claudia. *Almost 13*. Nashville, TN: Thomas Nelson Publishers, 1986.

Arp, Claudia, and Linda Dillow. *Sanity in the Summertime*. Nashville, TN: Thomas Nelson Publishers, 1981.

Arp, Dave, and Claudia Arp. *Ten Dates for Mates*. Nashville, TN: Thomas Nelson Publishers, 1983.

Campbell, Ross. *How to Really Love Your Child*. Wheaton, IL: Tyndale House Publishers, 1982.

Dobson, James. *The Strong-Willed Child*. Wheaton, IL: Tyndale House Publishers, 1988.

Kesler, Jay. *Parents and Teenagers*. Wheaton, IL: Victor Books, 1984.

King, Pat. *How to Have All the Time You Need Every Day*. Wheaton, IL: Tyndale House Publishers, 1980.

Liontos, Lynn, and Demetri Liontos. *The Good Couple Life. Winston-Salem, NC: The Association of Couples in Marriage Enrichment, Inc., 1982.*

McGinnis, Alan Loy. The Friendship Factor. Minneapolis, MN: Augsburg Publishing House, 1979.

Mace, David. *Close Companions: The Marriage Enhancement Handbook*. New York: Continuum, 1982.

Mace, David, and Vera Mace. *How to Have a Happy Marriage*. Nashville, TN: Abingdon Press, 1977.

_____. *Love and Anger in Marriage*. Grand Rapids, MI: Zondervan Publishing House, 1982.

Peterson, J. Alan. *The Marriage Affair*. Wheaton, IL: Tyndale House Publishers, 1974.

Ridenour, Fritz. *What Teenagers Wish Their Parents Knew About Kids*. Waco, TX: Word Publishers, 1982.

Sell, Charles. *Achieving the Impossible: Intimate Marriage*. New York: Ballentine, 1982.

Stanley, Phyllis, and Miltinnie Yih. *Celebrate the Seasons*. Colorado Springs, CO: Nav Press, 1986.

COLOPHON

The typeface for the text of this book is a modern version of *Goudy Oldstyle*, made more suitable for text typesetting because of a tighter set and a more subtle presentation of the distinctive flourishes that characterize it. Its creator, Frederick W. Goudy, was commissioned by American Type Founders Company to design a new Roman type face. Completed in 1915 and named Goudy Old Style, it was an instant bestseller. However, its designer had sold the design outright to the foundry, so when it became evident that additional versions would be needed to complete the family, the work was done by the foundry's own designer, Morris Benton. From the original design came seven additional weights and variants, all of which sold in great quantity. However, Goudy himself received no additional compensation for them. He later recounted a visit to the foundry with a group of printers, during which the guide stopped at one of the busy casting machines and stated, "Here's where Goudy goes down to posterity, while American Type Founders goes down to prosperity." The perfect blend of beauty and versatility of this classic and graceful design adds distinction wherever it's used. It is considered the most popular advertising typeface in use today.

Copy editing by Donna Sherwood
Cover design by Kent Puckett Associates, Atlanta, Georgia
Typography by Thoburn Press, Tyler, Texas
Printed and bound by Dickinson Press, Inc.
Grand Rapids, Michigan
Cover Printing by Weber Graphics, Chicago, Illinois